The Redneck Doesn't Fall Far from the Tree

Jeff Foxworthy

With illustrations by David Boyd

RUTLEDGE HILL PRESS
Nashville, Tennessee
A Division of Thomas Nelson Publishers
Since 1798

www.thomasnelson.com

Published by Rutledge Hill Press, a Division of Thomas Nelson, Inc., P.O. Box 141000, Nashville, Tennessee 37214.

Rutledge Hill Press books may be purchased in bulk for educational, business, fundraising, or sales promotional use. For information, please e-mail SpecialMarkets@ThomasNelson.com.

Library of Congress Cataloging-in-Publication Data

Foxworthy, Jeff.
    The redneck doesn't fall far from the tree / Jeff Foxworthy ; with illustrations by David Boyd.
        p. cm.
    ISBN 1-4016-0230-4 (pbk.)
    1. Rednecks—Humor. I. Title: Redneck does not fall far from the tree. II. Title.
PN6231.R38F6855 2006
818'.5402—dc22   2005036064

Printed in the United States of America

06 07 08 09 10 — 5 4 3 2 1

Introduction

In most families, it's not unusual to hear children described by their parents' physical traits: "He's got his daddy's eyes," or "He's got his mama's chin."

But in redneck families, when someone says, "He's got his daddy's jeans," they're not necessarily talking about DNA. They're probably talking about denim. If it was good enough for Daddy, it's good enough for his kids.

Unfortunately, redneck hand-me-downs aren't always limited to clothes. They often include such things as . . .

- Bad taste—naming a son for your favorite pro wrestler
- Bad habits—breaking wind in public and blaming your kids

- Poor judgment—teaching your kids how to make prank calls
- Rusted-out trucks—with bumper stickers that say, "Honk if you're horny!"
- Sorry-ness—a condition characterized by such actions as skipping your daughter's wedding because it fell on opening day of deer season, or taking the family to the Kmart electronics section to watch a movie
- Recessive chins—a sure sign that your family tree does not fork

The fact of the matter is that rednecks usually don't fall very far from the tree. And in some cases, when kissing cousins go too far, you can't even see a crack of daylight between them and the tree.

But it may not be fair to blame your ol' man for all your redneck habits. After all, he got them from his father who got them from his father who got them from . . . That's what some scientists and theologians refer to as "unintelligent design."

So when Father's Day rolls around, be kind to Dad. You'll be wearing his jeans before you know it

— **Jeff Foxworthy**

4

Your daddy tried to take you
fishing at Sea World.

You cried the day your son tapped his first keg.

6

You've ever changed a diaper on a Denny's table.

Your father fully executes the "pull my finger" trick during Christmas dinner.

8

You've ever been asked, "Daddy, why don't you marry Mommy?"

9

Any of your children
were conceived
in a bass boat.

You learned your father's real name while watching Unsolved Mysteries.

You got your picture taken sitting on Santa's knee, but your kids didn't.

12

Your baby's first words were
"Rack 'em!"

You use your daughter's wedding as an excuse to buy a new shotgun.

14

3

Your dad's most encouraging words are "Don't touch that, dipstick!"

15

Your father still gives wedgies.

You would rather
your son have his own
hunting show than
become a doctor.

17

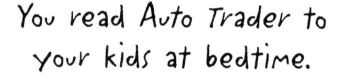

You read Auto Trader to your kids at bedtime.

18

Your daddy's headstone
includes the words
"worthless" and
"varmint."

You refer to your dog
as "my youngest."

20

Strangers mistakenly think
your children are already dressed
for trick or treat.

21

Your front yard
looks like Toys "R" Us
after a tornado.

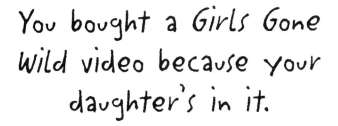

You bought a *Girls Gone Wild* video because your daughter's in it.

23

Your dad's cell number has nothing
to do with a telephone.

You've ever hunted within 20 yards of your child's swing set.

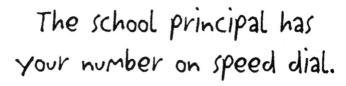

The school principal has your number on speed dial.

You carry a flyswatter in the front seat of the car so you can reach your kids in the back seat.

27

You spent a significant amount of your early years in the child care room at the bowling alley.

28

Your kids take roadkill
to show-and-tell.

You wear a beer-
dispensing hat to your
kid's Little League game.

30

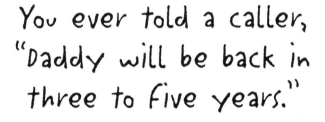

3

You ever told a caller,
"Daddy will be back in
three to five years."

31

Your daddy waves at traffic from
the front porch wearing nothing
but his underwear.

Your kids attend your high school graduation.

33

Your five-year-old can
rebuild a carburetor.

34

The giant box of kitchen matches on the back of the toilet was given to you by your children.

35

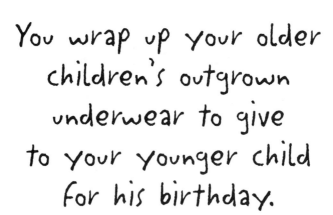

You wrap up your older
children's outgrown
underwear to give
to your younger child
for his birthday.

36

All your kids have
the middle name Elvis.

Your dogs understand
more commands than
your kids do.

According to your birth certificate, your father's name was X.

39

Your father ever had
to have his finger surgically
removed from his nose.

40

You tell your kids the facts of life and they interrupt you with corrections.

41

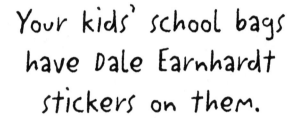

Your kids' school bags have Dale Earnhardt stickers on them.

You dated your
daddy's current wife
in high school.

43

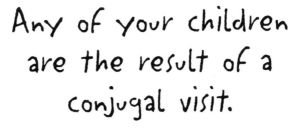

Any of your children are the result of a conjugal visit.

You know your daddy's CB handle
but not his real name.

45

3

You turn on your
sprinkler and tell your
kids it's a water park.

The kids are going hungry tonight because you just had to have those Yosemite Sam mud flaps.

47

Your kids trip over the Christmas
lights while hunting Easter eggs.

You punish your children by taking away their chewing tobacco.

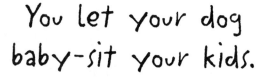

You let your dog
baby-sit your kids.

Your daughter refuses to drive your truck because of the "Honk if you're horny!" bumper sticker.

51

You've ever hollered, "You kids quit playing on that sheet metal!"

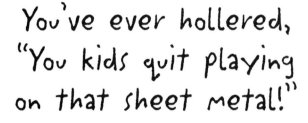

Your father's best shoes have
numbers on the back.

53

When describing your kids, you use the phrase "dumb as a brick."

54

Your daughter's
Barbie Dream House
has a clothesline
in the front yard.

55

You say your daddy lives in a gated community because he's in jail.

56

Your 14-year-old smokes
in front of her kids.

57

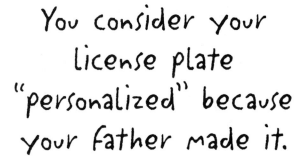

You consider your
license plate
"personalized" because
your father made it.

Your kid's favorite
bedtime story is
"Curious George and the
High-Voltage Fence."

59

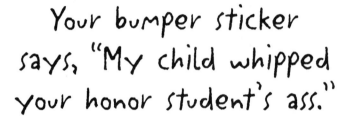

Your bumper sticker says, "My child whipped your honor student's ass."

You teach your kids how
to make prank phone calls.

All your kids' toys came free with a hamburger.

Your three-year-old is trained to bring a beer to any cops who show up at the door.

You've ever named a child
for a good dog.

You send your kid
in for treatment because
you think he's hooked
on phonics.

65

You named each of your
kids after the car they
were conceived in.

Baby-sitters never work for you more than once.

67

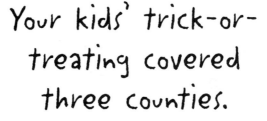

Your kids' trick-or-treating covered three counties.

68

The doctor who delivered your children also delivers your propane.

Your kid's birthday party activities included a rabbit-skinning contest.

You take the entire family to the Kmart electronics section to watch a movie.

You think the "six to ten pounds" on
the side of the Pampers box means
how much a diaper will hold.

Your kids have
a three-day-old
Kool-Aid mustache.

You break wind in public
and blame it on your kid.

Your daughter mistakenly thought you'd attend her wedding on opening day of deer season.

75

You taught your three-year-old
to give Jeff Gordon "the finger."

76

Your kids can't use
the sandbox because
the cats do.

77

Your kids can
demonstrate how
to rig a possum trap.

3

When the teacher asks your child, "What's your Dad like?" he answers, "Beer and Pamela Anderson."

79

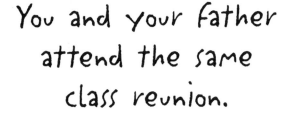

You and your father
attend the same
class reunion.

Your earliest childhood memory is
standing by the road while Dad
worked on the truck.

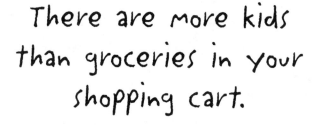

There are more kids
than groceries in your
shopping cart.

Your children catch frogs and lizards . . . inside the house.

83

You wear a giant foam finger at your child's graduation.

Your TV's remote control
is your son Junior.

Everyone in
the house learns
something from
the potty training
videotape.

Your son is named for your favorite pro wrestler.

87

Your dad taught you how to elude
a pack of trailing bloodhounds.

You wash your car more
often than your kids.

89

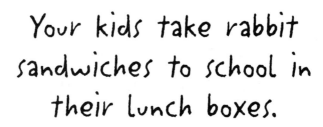

Your kids take rabbit
sandwiches to school in
their lunch boxes.

Any of your daughters
are older than your wife.

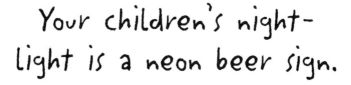

Your children's night-
light is a neon beer sign.

Your dad walks you to school
because you're in the same grade.

You know how to fit three baby seats into the back of a Trans Am.

You've ever hollered,
"Rock the house, Bubba!"
during your child's
piano recital.

Your two-year-old
has more teeth than you do.